Explore and Draw

HORSES

Ann Becker

www.rourkepublishing.com

Editor: Penny Dowdy
Art Direction: Tarang Saggar (Q2AMedia)
Designer: Neha Kaul (Q2AMedia)
Picture researcher: Jim Mathew (Q2AMedia)
Picture credits:
t=top b=bottom c=centre l=left r=right

Cover: Roma Oslo/Istockphoto.
Insides: Arfo/Istockphoto: 6, LesPalenik/Shutterstock: 7,
Zuzule/Shutterstock: 10, Tom Ervin/Getty Images: 11,
Robert Ranson/Shutterstock: 14, Alexia Khruscheva/Shutterstock: 15,
DEW/Bigstockphoto: 18, WILDLIFE GmbH/Alamy: 19,
Q2AMedia Art Bank: Cover, Title Page, 4, 5, 8, 9, 12, 13, 16, 17, 20, 21.
Every attempt has been made to clear copyright.
Should there be any inadvertent omission, please
apply to the publisher for rectification.

Library of Congress Cataloging-in-Publication Data

Becker, Ann, 1965 Oct. 6-
 Horses : explore and draw / Ann Becker.
    p. cm. -- (Explore and draw)
 Includes index.
 ISBN 978-1-60694-353-3 (hard cover)
 ISBN 978-1-60694-837-8 (soft cover)
1. Horses in art--Juvenile literature. 2. Drawing--Technique--Juvenile literature. I. Title. II. Title: Explore and draw.
 NC783.8.H65B43 2009
 743.6'96655--dc22

                                  2009021615

Printed in the USA
CG/CG

www.rourkepublishing.com - rourke@rourkepublishing.com
Post Office Box 643328 Vero Beach, Florida 32964

Contents

Technique

Proportion is comparing the size of one thing to another. Look at the horse's head. It is about half as long as the horse's neck. Using proportion helps the sizes look realistic.

1

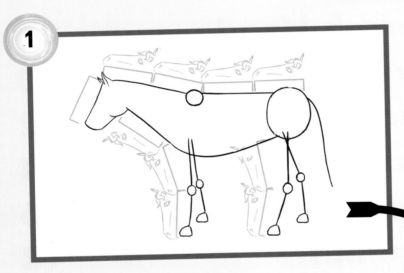

Find one part to compare against other parts. The size of a horse's head can be used to draw other parts of the body. The body is as long as four heads. The legs are as long as two heads.

2

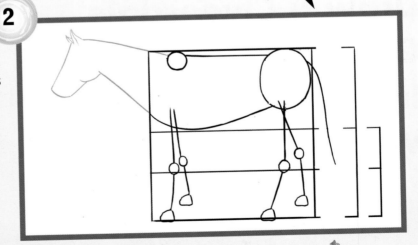

Compare the horse's body to its legs. The height of the horse's chest is the same as the length of its front legs.

3

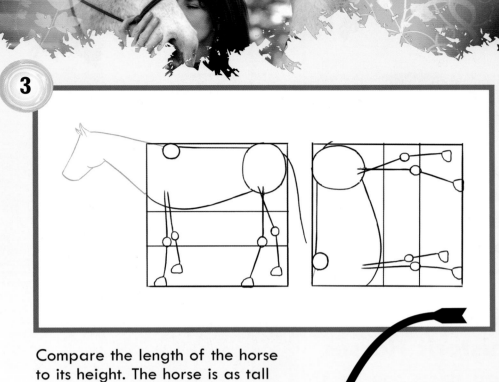

Compare the length of the horse to its height. The horse is as tall as the body is wide. Use a square to guide your drawings!

4

Make adjustments for specific horses. Some horses are longer and more rectangular. Others have shorter legs.

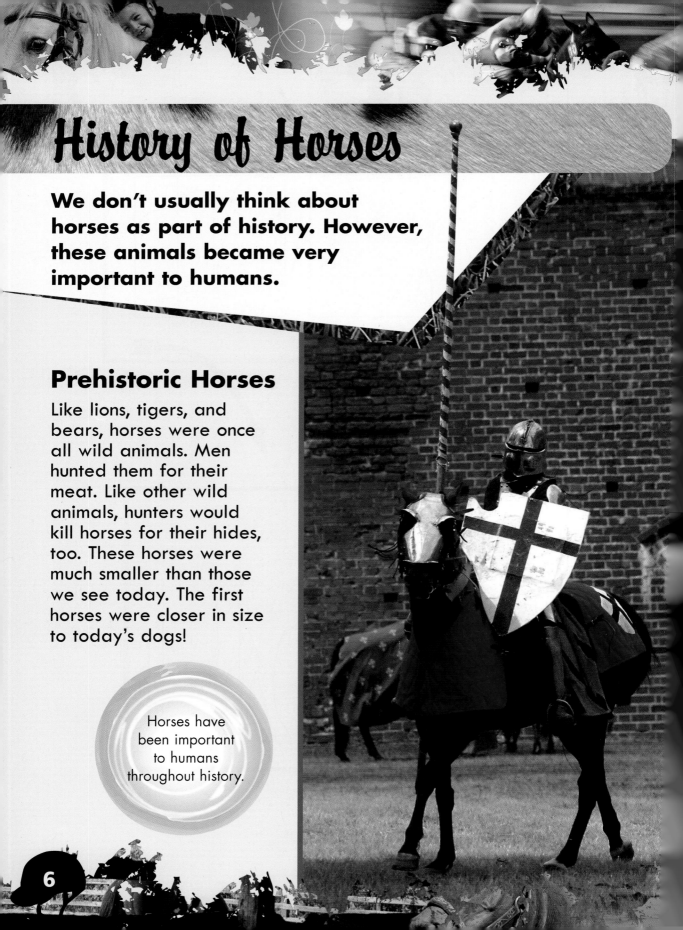

History of Horses

We don't usually think about horses as part of history. However, these animals became very important to humans.

Prehistoric Horses

Like lions, tigers, and bears, horses were once all wild animals. Men hunted them for their meat. Like other wild animals, hunters would kill horses for their hides, too. These horses were much smaller than those we see today. The first horses were closer in size to today's dogs!

Horses have been important to humans throughout history.

Horses help people in many ways, like pulling carriages.

Domesticating Horses

In about 4000 B.C., people in Asia found that they could **domesticate** horses. A tame horse was very valuable! It could carry or pull things. **Merchants** could use the horses to carry their goods. Farmers could have horses plow their fields.

But remember that the horses were small. People started **breeding** horses to grow larger and stronger. Bigger, more powerful horses could carry and pull more.

Bringing Horses to New Lands

Some parts of the world did not have horses. When peddlers brought their goods on horseback to new places, some left the horses behind. Slowly, horses came to every corner of the world.

These horses became vital to people's daily lives. They pulled carriages to move people from place to place. They carried soldiers into battle. If an army had access to horses, they were immediately more powerful than an army that did not. Until cars and airplanes came along, horses were as important as weapons in war.

Draw a Horse's Head

You can use proportion to draw a horse's head. Remember to look at the sizes of different parts of your drawing.

1 The front of the horse's head is about the same length as the back of its neck. The nose is narrower, so use the two circles to get the size right.

2 Turn your lines and shapes into a more accurate horse. Ears are at the top, its jaw curves near the neck, and the lips are at the very bottom.

8

3 The horse's mane grows around the ears and down the neck. Add the nostril just above the lips.

4 Notice that the eye is about the size of the nostril. This is using proportion, too. After you add the eye, spend time on details of the face and mane.

5 You're doing great. To make your drawing more lifelike, add some shading to the face and neck.

How Horses Live

All horses were once wild animals. Today, most horses live with people.

In the Wild

Some horses still live in the wild. In the United States, about 37,000 horses live in places such as national parks and **undeveloped** lands. In the early 1900s, the U.S. had over a million wild horses!

Wild horses live in wide open spaces.

Working Horses

Today most horses live with and help people in many different ways. Ranchers use horses to ride with herds of cattle. The horses can also travel on land where trucks and cars can't go. Therapy horses can assist people who are ill or have disabilities. People develop muscles and other skills riding and caring for horses.

You may have seen police officers riding horses. They give police an **advantage**. The riders sit high off the ground and can see into traffic and crowds well.

This child strengthens his muscles and improves his balance working with horses!

Horses in Sports

Horses work with people in sports, too. Race horses have great speed. The best race horses are worth millions of dollars. Other sports include polo, jumping, and **dressage**.

Draw a Horse Running

When a horse runs, some proportions stay the same, and others change.

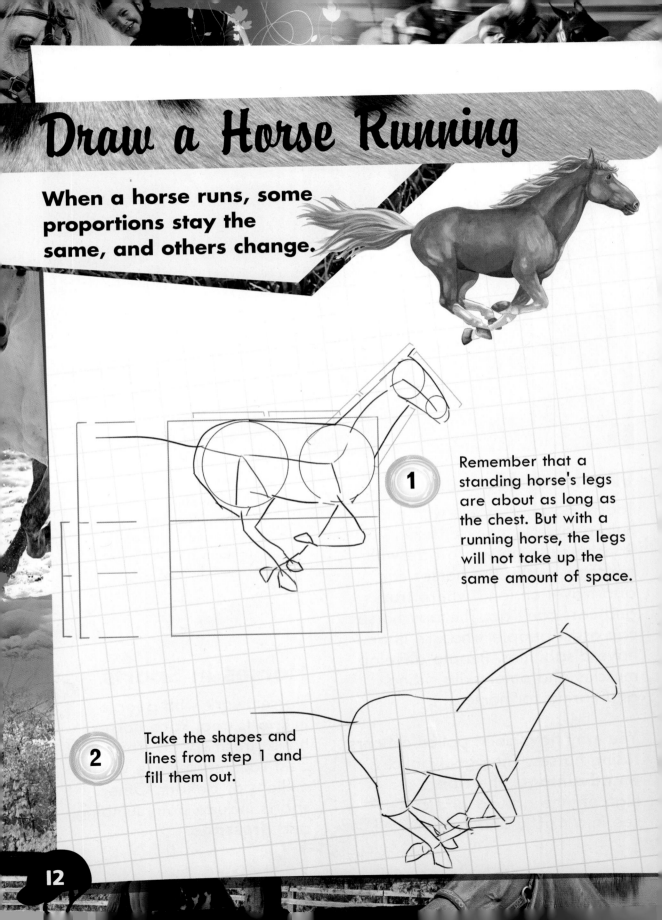

1 Remember that a standing horse's legs are about as long as the chest. But with a running horse, the legs will not take up the same amount of space.

2 Take the shapes and lines from step 1 and fill them out.

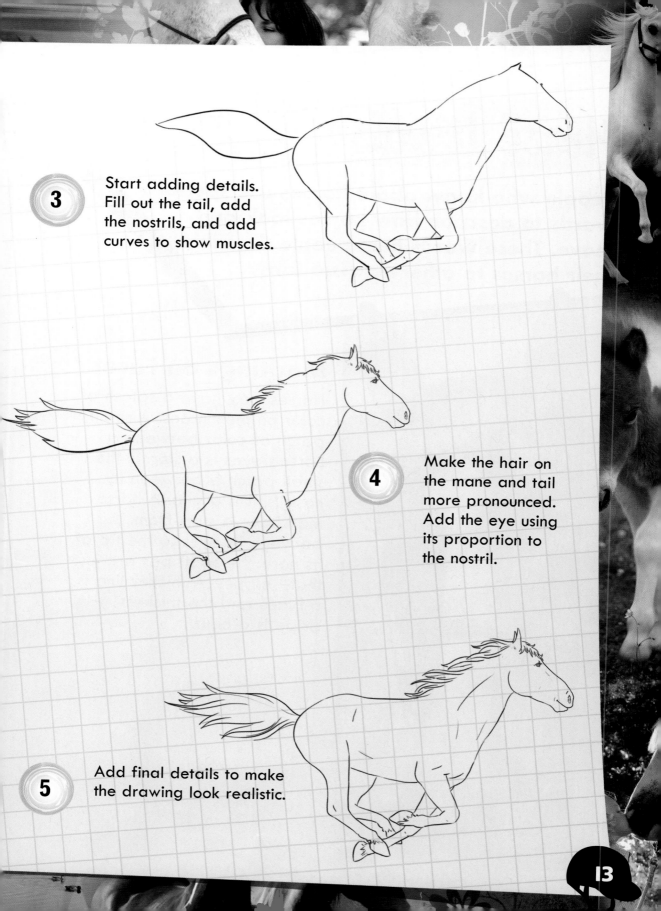

3 Start adding details. Fill out the tail, add the nostrils, and add curves to show muscles.

4 Make the hair on the mane and tail more pronounced. Add the eye using its proportion to the nostril.

5 Add final details to make the drawing look realistic.

Horse Words

People who know about horses use special words to describe how horses look and move. These words help people describe their horses to other **equine** fans.

Markings on Faces

Horses may have a splash of color on their noses. A small patch of color between a horse's eyes is a *star*. If the small patch is between its nostrils, it is a *snip*. A horse may have a strip from between its eyes to the tip of its nose. These stripes are just that—*stripes*. A thicker line is a *blaze* and the thickest stripe is a *bald*.

This thick stripe is a bald.

Markings on Legs

Horses might have marks on their legs, too. The shortest marks are *coronets*. As these marks get closer to the knee, they change from *half pasterns* to *socks* and *half cannons*. Horses with the longest marks from the foot to the knee are wearing *stockings*. A horse might have a coronet on one leg, a half cannon on another, a sock on the third, and a stocking on the fourth!

How Horses Move

Just like there are words for markings, people use special words for movement. A walk is slow, with a *one-two-three-four* beat. A trot is faster: *one-two, one-two*. As the horse speeds up, the pattern changes to *one-two-three, one-two-three*. This is a gallop.

This horse trots with a one-two, one-two beat.

Draw a Horse with Markings

As you get better at drawing horses, add details like markings on its feet and face.

1 This horse is standing, so the first proportions you used will work here.

2 Use the sketch of shapes from step 1 to fill out the shape of the horse's body.

3 Here, spend time on the horse's face and mane. Notice how the eye lines up with the nostril.

4 Now make your horse unique. This horse has a blaze. What mark does your horse have? This horse has stockings. How are your horse's feet marked?

5 Finish your drawing with shadows and details to make it realistic.

Unusual Equines

Horses come in all shapes and sizes. Some horse owners prefer to own unusual horses instead of the typical horse you think of.

This horse is a miniature. It will never be big enough to ride.

Miniatures

Just like some horses were bred to become larger and stronger, others were bred to become smaller. Miniature horses can be as small as 20 pounds and less than two feet tall! Just like dogs, miniature horses can be trained as guides for disabled people.

Gaited Horses

Gaited horses have an unusual way of walking. They can walk, trot, and gallop, but they have some other fancy steps, too. Paso Finos come from Spain. They have a special gait that looks like a high step. Even though their legs move differently, riding a Paso Fino is very smooth.

Walking horses have an unusual gait, too. They have a running walk, where their heads bob and ears swing. When they gallop, it looks like a rocking chair rocking back and forth!

Draft Horses

Remember that people domesticated horses so that they could pull or carry things. Some breeders made very large horses to carry and pull extra-large loads. Draft horses are tall, muscular horses bred to work. They pulled heavy weapons in war hundreds of years ago. Today they pull wagons and plows.

A Paso Fino has an unusual walk, or gait. The front legs kick high as they step, but the back legs do not kick up at all.

Draw a Clydesdale

A Clydesdale is a draft horse. They are one of the strongest animals on Earth!

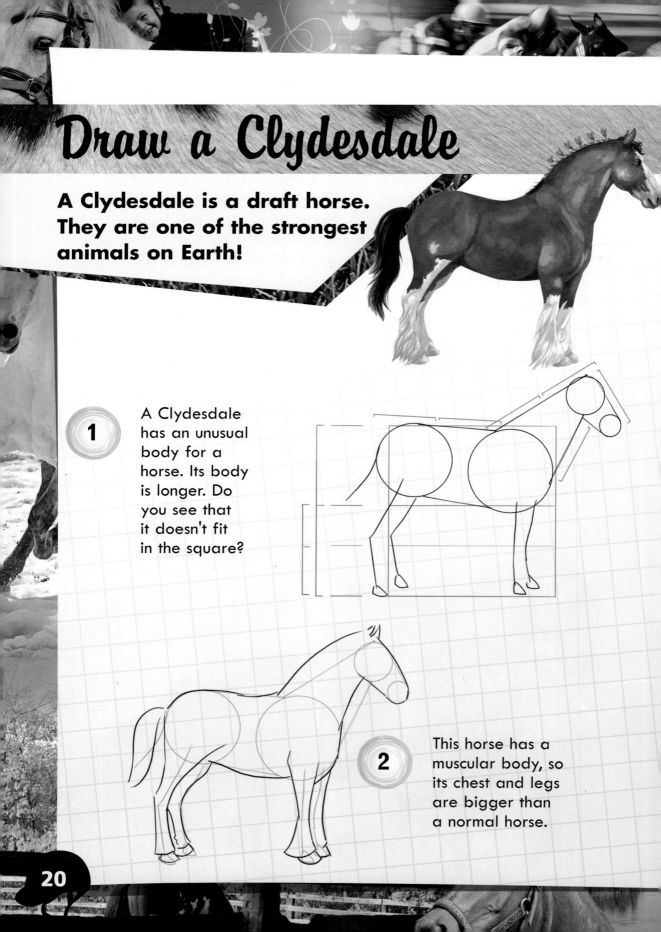

1 A Clydesdale has an unusual body for a horse. Its body is longer. Do you see that it doesn't fit in the square?

2 This horse has a muscular body, so its chest and legs are bigger than a normal horse.

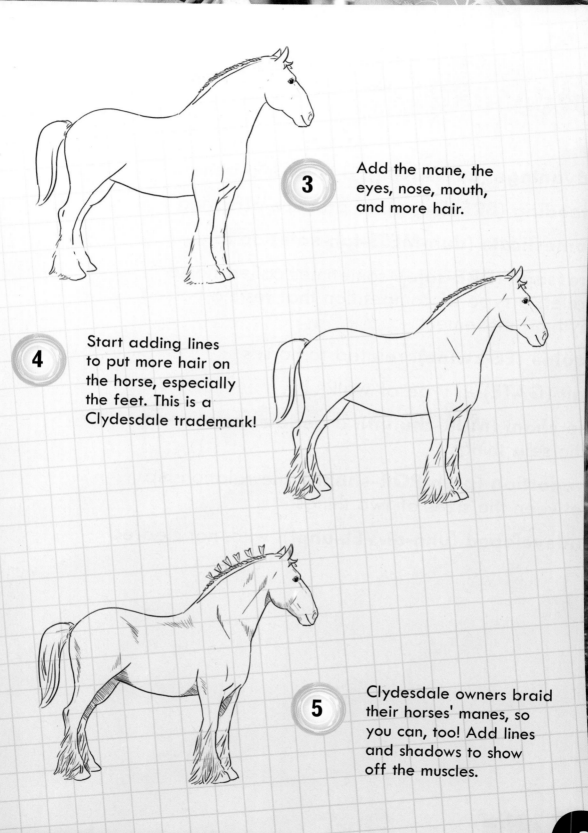

3 Add the mane, the eyes, nose, mouth, and more hair.

4 Start adding lines to put more hair on the horse, especially the feet. This is a Clydesdale trademark!

5 Clydesdale owners braid their horses' manes, so you can, too! Add lines and shadows to show off the muscles.

Glossary

advantage (ad-VAN-tij): a help or a benefit

breeding (BREED-ing): to produce offspring

domesticate (duh-MESS-tuh-kate): to tame

dressage (DRE-saje): sometimes called horse ballet, a type of competition that tests a horse's rhythmic movement

equine (EE-kwine): related to horses

gait (GATE): a type of walk

merchant (MUR-chuhnt): a peddler or someone who sells things

proportion (pruh-POR-shuhn): the relationship between the sizes of two things

undeveloped (uhn-di-VEL-uhpt): wild, not cleared

Index

Websites

www.horsefun.com/
A website for kids who love horses.

www.amnh.org/exhibitions/horse/
The American Museum of Natural History's online
exhibit on horses.

www.amha.org/
A website for the American Miniature Horse Association.

www.dirjournal.com/kids/arts/drawing/
A cool website which contains stories, art, and comparisons.

http://ultimatehorsefun.com/
A website with games, crafts, stories, and jokes about horses.

http://animals.howstuffworks.com/mammals/horse-info16.htm
A website which provides an explanation of what happens at
a horse show.

About the Author
Ann Becker is an avid reader. Ann likes to read books, magazines,
and even Internet articles. She hopes that someday she will get
to go on a game show and put all of that reading to good use!

About the Illustrator
Maria Menon has been illustrating children's books for almost
a decade. She loves making illustrations of animals, especially
dragons and dinosaurs. She is fond of pets and has two dogs
named Spot and Lara. When she is not busy illustrating, Maria
spends her time watching animated movies.

DATE DUE
